# JUSTICE

Terrorists don't care who they kill or hurt; they're not interested in justice for other people, only in bombs and guns and killing – and in escaping from the law themselves. But there is another kind of justice, an older kind, before there were police and laws and prisons. It's called an eye for an eye, a tooth for a tooth, a life for a life . . .

The bomb goes off in the Queen's coach outside Parliament, killing five people, and only just missing the Queen. Jane Cole is watching from the crowd. Her father was driving the Queen's coach, and now Jane, sick with fear, pushes through the terrified crowd to look for him. She finds him lying on the ground, covered in blood and screaming in pain.

Alan Cole lives, but he loses his leg. And the terror for him and his daughter is only just beginning, because Alan knows something about the terrorists. He hasn't realized it yet, but he soon will.

And somebody, somewhere, desperately wants to stop Alan Cole realizing . . . and talking.

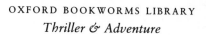

OXFORD BOOKWORMS LIBRARY
*Thriller & Adventure*

# Justice

Stage 3 (1000 headwords)

Series Editor: Jennifer Bassett
Founder Editor: Tricia Hedge
Activities Editors: Jennifer Bassett and Christine Lindop

TIM VICARY

# Justice

OXFORD UNIVERSITY PRESS

Oxford University Press
Great Clarendon Street, Oxford OX2 6DP

Oxford New York

Athens Auckland Bangkok Bogotá Buenos Aires Calcutta Cape Town
Chennai Dar es Salaam Delhi Florence Hong Kong Istanbul Karachi
Kuala Lumpur Madrid Melbourne Mexico City Mumbai Nairobi
Paris São Paulo Shanghai Singapore Taipei Tokyo Toronto Warsaw
and associated companies in
Berlin Ibadan

OXFORD and OXFORD ENGLISH
are trade marks of Oxford University Press

ISBN  0 19 423005 8

© Oxford University Press 2000

Third impression 2001

First published in Oxford Bookworms 1995
This second edition published in the Oxford Bookworms Library 2000

Illustrated by Chris Chaisty

Typeset by Wyvern Typesetting Ltd, Bristol
Printed in Spain

# CONTENTS

# 1
# BOMB

'Look!' Jane Cole said. 'Here she comes now!'

The two Americans looked along the street. There were crowds of people everywhere. In the middle of the road, soldiers were riding towards them on horseback. Behind them came a golden coach, pulled by six black horses.

'That's my father,' Jane said. 'He's the coachman – the man driving the horses.'

The American woman said: 'Fantastic! Your father's driving the Queen! Quick, Harry, use the video camera!'

'I *am* using it!' her husband said. 'But she's too far away. Can't we get a little nearer, Jane?'

'We can try,' Jane said. 'Follow me!' She took them nearer to the entrance to Parliament. 'This is where the coach will stop and the Queen will get out. Then she'll go upstairs to open Parliament for this year.'

'Didn't someone put a bomb under your Parliament once?' the American man asked. 'I read about that at school. Guy . . . something?'

'Guy Fawkes,' Jane said. 'In 1605. He tried to blow up Parliament, that's right. But don't worry. There's no Guy Fawkes here today.'

She smiled at the Americans. She was a student, and this was her part-time job – to show tourists round London.

She felt proud to show them her father, driving the Queen on a wonderful day like this.

Then the Queen's coach came past in front of them, the golden roof bright in the sunlight.

There were people everywhere, trying to take photos. Jane saw a woman with red-brown hair behind the American man, pressing the button of her camera. That's stupid, Jane thought; she can only see the backs of people's heads there. The woman shook her camera angrily; there seemed to be something wrong with it. The American woman pulled Jane forward, laughing happily. 'Come on,' she said, 'let's get to the front! Use that video, Harry!'

Alan Cole stopped the coach outside Parliament, and sat there, quietly holding the horses. A man opened the coach door, and Prince Charles and the Duke of Edinburgh got out. Then the Queen got out. She was wearing a long white dress, and carrying a gold handbag. She walked slowly towards the entrance to the building.

'Excuse me, please,' the woman with red-brown hair said. 'I must get closer.' She pushed past Jane and held out her small black camera.

'Oh, all right,' Jane said. 'But . . . *my God!*'

There was a loud BANG! Jane saw a bright white light in front of her eyes, and felt a terrible hot wind on her face. The wind threw her backwards, and she fell to the ground with a lot of other people. For a moment she lay there, not thinking, not seeing.

Her eyes were open but she saw nothing. Only . . . blue

*The woman shook her camera angrily.*

sky. She heard nothing. Only . . . silence. Her body felt no pain. But she could smell something. Smoke.

Smoke? she thought. I don't understand. Why smoke? And this blue sky. Where am I?

Then the screaming began.

The screaming was high and loud and terrible. It didn't sound human. It went on and on and on.

Jane saw a hand in front of her, on the ground. A man's hand with blood on it. And broken glass. She moved her head and saw broken glass everywhere, and blood, and bodies lying on the ground. She stood up slowly.

For a moment she thought everyone was dead. There were bodies everywhere, but no one was moving. Then a man ran across the road, and one of the bodies moved.

The body wasn't human; it was a horse. As it moved, it screamed. The horse tried to stand up, but it couldn't, because it only had three legs. There was blood all round the horse, and a big bit of wood in its stomach.

The Queen's coach was broken into a thousand pieces, and there were bits of wood and clothes and bodies everywhere. The bodies looked like broken dolls.

'Dad!' she screamed. 'Oh God – *my father*!'

She ran quickly towards the coach. A policeman with a bloody hand tried to stop her, but she pushed him away.

'My father's over there!' she screamed.

At first she couldn't find him. There were so many bodies – and so much blood! She saw the horse in the middle of a great lake of blood, trying to get up on its front leg. There was blood coming from the horse's nose and stomach – and under the back legs, something that looked like . . .

A body. A man. '*Father!*'

Alan Cole was covered with blood and his face was as white as paper. When he saw Jane, he opened his eyes and screamed. 'It's my leg! My leg – get this horse off me!'

His leg was under the back of the horse, which was moving wildly, trying to get up. Each time the horse moved, it fell on Alan Cole's leg, and he screamed.

Jane ran and pushed the horse but it was too big, too heavy. She pulled its tail but that was no good. It tried to get up and fell on her father's leg again, twice. She could hear his bones breaking. Then a policeman came and held the horse's leg. Jane held its tail, and another policeman held Alan's arms. Jane and the first policeman pulled the horse to one side, while the second policeman pulled Alan free. The horse screamed, kicked Jane on the shoulder, and died.

• • •

Jane went in the ambulance with her father to the hospital. There were lots of people there. She heard a reporter talking on the telephone to his office.

'Five,' he said. 'Five dead, and about thirty are very badly hurt. It was a bomb – it must be terrorists. But the Queen is safe. She was inside Parliament with her husband and Prince Charles and . . .'

'Never mind the bloody Queen!' Jane thought. 'What about my father!'

The doctors took Alan away from Jane, and she had to

'*Get this horse off me!*'

sit and wait. Her shoulder was hurt, but not badly. For nearly four hours she walked up and down, drank coffee, and thought: *why?*

Why try to kill the Queen – how will that help anyone? Why kill tourists and soldiers outside Parliament? *Why try to kill my father?*

Jane's father was the most important person in the world to her. When he was a soldier, she had travelled around the world with him. He had taught her to climb mountains, win judo fights, ride horses, sail boats – he was a great father. Now, she thought, he may be dead.

At midnight, a young Indian doctor came to see her. He was tired and serious. He looked at her sadly.

'It's bad news, isn't it?' Jane said. 'Is he dead?'

'No, Miss Cole,' the doctor said. 'We have saved your father's life. But I am afraid . . .' He hesitated.

'Yes? What then? Please – tell me!'

'I am afraid he has lost his leg. It was too badly broken – we had to cut it off.'

'Oh my God!' Jane sat down suddenly. 'You cut his leg off!' She stared at the doctor and thought: Dad will never be able to climb or ride or sail again. Oh, poor man! It's worse than being dead! She began to cry.

'I'm very sorry, miss,' the doctor said. 'We had to do it, to save his life. He'll get an artificial leg. He'll learn to use it. At least he's alive . . .'

'Yes, I suppose so.' Jane looked up. 'I'm sorry, doctor. I'm sure you did your best. Can I see him now?'

'Yes, of course. The nurse will show you . . .'

In the hospital bed, Alan Cole lay quietly. His face was as white as the sheets on the bed, but when Jane came in, he opened his eyes slowly. Jane took one of his hands in hers. The hand was cold, like ice.

'Janie? Are you all right?'

'Me? I'm fine, Dad. And you're going to be OK too, aren't you? The doctor told me.'

He closed his eyes, and for a long time he didn't answer. Perhaps he's asleep again, Jane thought. Then, very quietly, Alan Cole said: 'Stay with me, Janie.'

'Of course, Dad. I'm not going anywhere.' Jane sat down on a chair beside the bed. 'You sleep now.'

Her father closed his eyes, and the nurse smiled at Jane. 'Would you like a cup of tea, miss?'

'Yes, please,' Jane said. 'It's going to be a long night.' She held her father's hand, and watched him sleeping. He looks happy now, she thought. Like a baby.

But what will he say when I tell him about the leg?

• • •

Next day, the doctor told Alan about his leg. Jane sat by the bed and held his hand while he listened. He didn't say anything, but tears came into his eyes.

'I'm very sorry, Mr Cole,' the doctor said. 'But we had to do it. Your leg was broken in forty places, and you lost a lot of blood. You're lucky to be alive.'

'Lucky!' Alan Cole said angrily. 'With this? Damn it, man, I'll never walk again!'

'Oh yes, you will, Mr Cole. We'll get you an artificial leg. They're very good – they move like an ordinary leg. No one will see it under your trousers.'

'And will I be able to ride horses with it, or swim, or climb mountains?'

'Well, perhaps not . . .' The doctor hesitated. 'We'll do our best for you, Mr Cole, believe me. Now, here's something to help you sleep. You'll feel better later.'

All day, Jane waited in the hospital. She drank tea, read newspapers, had a meal, and held her father's hand as he slept. No one came to visit. Her mother was dead, and her brother lived in Australia. At four o'clock her father woke up, and looked at her with big frightened eyes.

'Janie?' he said.

'Yes, Dad.'

'What happened? The doctor said there was a bomb, didn't he? And I lost my leg. But . . . I can't remember.'

Very quietly, Jane told him what she had seen. Then she read the newspaper aloud.

Five people have died, and forty are in hospital. One man from the Queen's coach lost a leg, and the other three are dead. But the Queen, Prince Charles, and the Duke of Edinburgh were not hurt. Yesterday some Irish terrorists rang the BBC to say they exploded the bomb. 'We are sorry that ordinary people died,' they said. 'We meant to kill the Queen, not them. But accidents happen sometimes. The Queen was lucky this time, because the bomb exploded

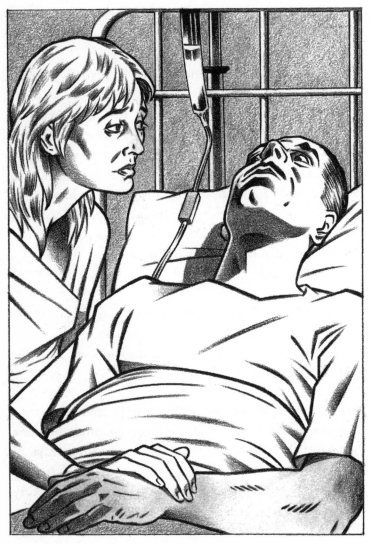

*Jane stroked her father's hand softly.*

too late. But *she* has to be lucky every time. *We* only have to be lucky once.'

'My God!' Alan said. 'The bastards! Who . . . who died?'

'One policeman, a tourist, and three coachmen,' Jane said. 'You were the only coachman who didn't die.'

'Oh no.' Alan's eyes filled with tears. 'George, Bernard, John – dead! What harm had they ever done to the Irish, or to anyone? Why did the Irish have to kill *them* with their bloody bomb? There's no justice in this life, is there?'

'Well, perhaps the police will . . .' Jane began.

'Yes, I hope they catch those murdering Irish bastards, I really do. I hope they lock them in prison until they die. That's what I hope. By God, I do!'

'Of course they will, Dad.' Jane stroked her father's hand softly. 'The police are out there now, looking for the bombers. They'll catch them, before too long.'

## 2

## Anna

That night Alan was moved to another hospital, where they would fit him with an artificial leg. Jane went with him and slept in a visitor's room there. In the morning she bought a newspaper. She was right about the police. 'They've got them, Dad!' she said. 'Read this!'

**Police yesterday arrested two Irishmen who they think**

put a bomb in the Queen's coach last week. The police said: 'Last week the coach went to a factory in south London to have new wheels fitted, and we believe the bomb was placed in the coach there. The two Irishmen worked at this factory, and two days before the bombing, they went on holiday to Ireland. We think the bomb had a clock in it, which was meant to explode at eleven o'clock outside Parliament. Luckily for the Queen, the bomb exploded after she had left the coach.'

Alan Cole put the newspaper down slowly. He looked pleased. 'Thank God for that,' he said.

'But why did they want the bomb to explode outside Parliament?' Jane asked. 'The Queen was in the coach for twenty minutes – why not blow the coach up earlier?'

'I don't know. Perhaps they wanted good pictures on TV,' Alan said. 'It was lucky for the Queen. But not lucky for me, or for the poor people who were killed.'

'No.' Jane put her hand on her father's, and remembered those minutes outside Parliament. The American man using his video camera, and the woman with red-brown hair shaking her camera angrily. Then . . . she shut her eyes, and saw the smoke, and the horse screaming, and the blood and bodies everywhere . . .

What kind of people could do that?

'I suppose the terrorists watched it on TV,' she said. 'They were in Ireland when the bomb exploded.'

'I expect they did,' Alan said. 'I expect they were laughing

12

as people died. But I'm pleased the police have caught them. Now perhaps they'll leave me alone.'

'Who? The police? Dad, what do you mean?'

Alan sighed. 'Well, yesterday they came to ask me about the night before the bombing. I went back to the Mews at about ten o'clock that night, you know, to look at a horse with a bad leg. I often do that. They asked if I saw anything strange, or looked at the coach.'

'And what did you tell them?'

Alan looked angry. 'What do you think, Jane? Of course I saw nothing strange! I was looking at the horse, not the coach. And we were only there half an hour.'

'*We*, Dad?' Jane asked. 'Was someone with you?'

Alan hesitated. 'Well, yes . . . a lady friend of mine, Anna. You haven't met her, Jane, but I've told her about you. She's nice, you'll like her. She sometimes comes to see the horses with me.'

Jane felt embarrassed. After her mother had died four years ago, Jane had lived at home with her father. Once, he had brought a woman home to the house, but Jane had had a terrible argument with her, and the woman had left. There had been no other women, until Jane left home to go to university. Now . . .?

Well, her father was an adult, of course he could have women friends. But Jane hated it. She had loved her mother too much. And she loved her father too.

'What kind of a woman is she?' she asked angrily.

He's *my* father, she thought – I don't want another woman

13

taking him away from me.

'Tall. Pretty. Red-brown hair. She likes horses and . . . films. We go to the cinema a lot.'

'Is she in love with you?'

'Well . . . perhaps, Janie, I don't know. I've only known her a few weeks. You'll like her, Janie, she's good fun.'

Jane was still angry, she couldn't stop herself. 'Then why isn't she here? Why hasn't she come to visit you?'

Now Alan looked embarrassed. 'Well, I was going to ask you, Janie . . . she doesn't have a phone, you see, and . . . perhaps she thinks I'm dead, like the others. God knows what she'll think of a man with one leg, but I do want to see her . . . so I've written this letter. Could you post it for me, Janie? Please?'

Jane took the letter and read the address. *Anna Barry, 14 Bowater Gardens, London NE11.*

'Dad, your name was in the newspapers. This woman can read, can't she? She must know you're alive.'

'Yes, but . . . perhaps she doesn't know which hospital. I don't know. Janie, please – don't be difficult.'

'Have you told the police about this woman, Dad?'

'Not yet.'

'Why not? They'll ask her questions, won't they?'

Alan sighed. 'Yes, I suppose so. I warned her about that in the letter. Perhaps that's why she hasn't come. You see . . . it's a bit difficult, Janie. Anna has a husband . . . and so it will be embarrassing for her if he finds out about us. Perhaps the police will want to ask her husband questions, too, and

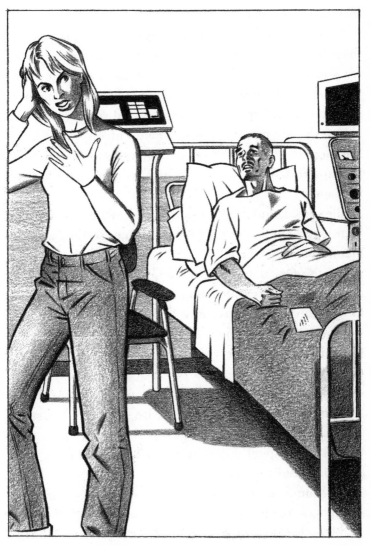

*'It's a bit difficult, Janie. Anna has a husband.'*

then there'll be all kinds of trouble.'

'I see,' Jane said. She felt miserable. My own father, she thought, in love with a married woman. Then she saw the tears in his eyes, and his tired white face; and felt angry with herself, not him. Why shouldn't my father fall in love, she thought? It happens to everyone, and you can't always choose the best person. Now he's here with only one leg and I'm angry with him. I'm his daughter, I should help him! Perhaps this Anna really is a nice woman, with a cruel husband.

She smiled, and said: 'I'm sorry, Dad. Of course I'll post your letter. But . . . isn't it a bit dangerous, sending a letter? Her husband could read it.'

'No, it's OK. Bowater Gardens is just where she's living at the moment. It isn't her home. I don't know where her husband lives. I don't want to know.' He smiled and took her hand. 'She's a lovely woman, Janie, really she is. You'll like her if you meet her, you know.'

• • •

Outside the hospital, Jane walked slowly down the street. She felt sad, and a little lonely. I wish my mother was still alive, she thought. I wish Mum was alive now, sitting with Dad in the hospital. I don't want all these problems. Why does Dad need another woman?

Oh Mum, why did you die? I need someone to talk to.

She took the letter out of her pocket and looked at it. I wonder what this Anna Barry is like, she thought. Perhaps she *is* nice, like Dad says. Perhaps I could talk to *her*. Perhaps she really does love Dad; perhaps *she* can help me look after him.

But why hasn't she come to see him?

She looked at the address again. 14 Bowater Gardens, London NE11. That wasn't far from her own student flat.

Why not take the letter myself? she thought. Then, if this Anna opens the door, I can talk to her myself. If I meet her, at least I'll find out what she's like.

Jane put the letter in her bag and walked quickly to the underground station. Am I full of anger, she wondered. Or hope?

• • •

14 Bowater Gardens was an old house in a quiet street in north London. Jane took the letter out of her bag, and rang the bell. Nothing happened.

Damn! she thought. She rang again. Still no answer. She tried the door, but it was locked. So she put the letter through the letter-box and turned away. Then she stopped.

I've come all this way to meet this woman, Jane thought, and I want to know what she's like. She's important to my father so she's important to me. I'll wait.

As she stood there, a woman came out of the house next door. She had grey hair and the kind of face that enjoys watching the neighbours and talking about them.

'They've gone; there's no use waiting,' the woman said. 'I saw you ring the bell so I came to tell you.'

'Are you sure?' Jane said. 'I was looking for Anna.'

'The girl with red hair? That's right, she did live here, but

she moved out with her boyfriend two days ago. It was the
morning of that terrible bomb – that's why I remember it.
The house is empty now. I had a look through the windows,

*'They've gone; there's no use waiting.'*

and they've taken everything.'

*Boyfriend!* So Anna had another lover, Jane thought. Not just Dad. My poor, poor father!

'Did you know them well?' the woman asked.

'No, not really,' Jane said. 'I just wanted to . . .'

'They were only here about three months,' the woman went on. 'They weren't very friendly. Never said good morning or anything like that. They were Irish, I think. Well, he was. There's a lot of Irish around here.'

Jane began to move away from the door, and the woman added, helpfully, 'Perhaps your friend will write to you.'

'Yes. Perhaps.' Jane smiled at her and walked sadly down the street.

So that was the kind of woman Anna was. She probably never loved my father at all, Jane thought. How am I going to tell him? Poor Dad! Perhaps I'll just say that I posted the letter, and not tell him that I came to the house and found out about her.

But Jane wasn't very good at lying, and she didn't want to look at her father's sad eyes and tired white face. Let him hope for a few more hours, she thought. I'll go home now and tell him something tomorrow.

She hadn't been back to her flat since the bombing. She loved having her own home. It was only one big bedroom really, with a small bathroom and kitchen. But it was her own place; she could do what she liked there.

She shut the door, then took off her coat and threw it on the bed. Then she heard the bathroom door slowly open behind her. She jumped round, her heart beating fast with fear, and saw a woman standing in the doorway!

'Who the hell are you?' she screamed. A thief, she thought. Jane had learned judo from her father; she knew what to do. She grabbed the woman's arm and threw her towards the bed. But as the woman fell, she grabbed Jane's hair, pulling it forwards, to stop herself from falling. Jane screamed, and pushed a hand into the woman's face, harder and harder until her hair was free. Then she hit the woman in the face and she fell to the floor. Jane stepped back, looked at her, and saw . . .

A man coming out of the kitchen. He had cold grey eyes and a thin hard smile and worst of all he had a gun in his hand. He said: 'Don't.'

Jane stood still, shaking. 'Don't what?'

'Move. Or talk. Don't do anything.' The little black hole in the end of the gun watched her, like a cold eye.

The woman got up off the floor, pulled Jane onto a chair, and tied her hands behind her. Then Jane remembered that there were people in the other flats, and opened her mouth to scream. The man hit her in the face.

'Don't even think about it,' he said. He took a long piece of cloth out of his pocket and tied it twice round her head, covering her mouth and the lower part of her face. Jane felt her body shaking with fear. Who were these people? What did they want with her? She stared at the man's cold hard face, the woman's blue eyes and red-brown hair. She thought she had seen the woman before. But where?

*Who were these people? What did they want with her?*

The woman tied Jane's legs to the chair. The little black eye of the gun was only a few centimetres from her face. The man watched her and smiled. 'Just sit still and be sensible, little girl,' he said. 'Then perhaps you'll live a few hours longer.'

## 3

## 'I made him happy'

Alan Cole lay in his bed, listening to a bird singing in the hospital garden. It was nearly dark outside now, and very quiet. He liked to lie like this, remembering.

He remembered the way Anna had kissed him, and looked into his eyes. He remembered her red-brown hair, her blue eyes, the soft, dry touch of her lips, her deep, happy laugh. She liked to drink whisky before they made love, and afterwards, she often held his head on her chest and stroked his hair.

I loved that, he remembered. I felt like a child again, safe and comfortable. Sometimes I fell asleep.

And then what? On the night before the bombing, he and Anna had been out for a meal in a restaurant. Then they had gone to the Mews to look at the horses. The guards knew she was his girlfriend, so they didn't think it was unusual. One of the horses, Sandman, had hurt his leg that morning, Alan remembered. In the evening the leg had been hot, so he had put ice on it. Lucky Sandman, he thought – he couldn't pull

They had gone to the Mews to look at the horses.

the coach next day, so he was still alive now.

Afterwards they went back to his house and made love. Anna had been very excited, Alan remembered; it had been very good. Then he had slept until morning. He woke at six o'clock and dressed quietly, but she woke up just before he left. She opened her eyes, smiled at him, and held out her arms to him sleepily. He kissed her, and she said: 'Goodbye, lover.'

That was the last time he had seen her.

He was still thinking about Anna when he drove the Queen's coach to Parliament, with the six fine horses in front of him. For a moment he thought he saw her in the crowd, watching . . .

Alan didn't want to think about what had happened next. He stared into the darkness outside the hospital window and thought: why hasn't she come to see me?

Perhaps she never really loved me, he thought. Perhaps she's gone back to her husband, or found a younger man. It's cruel and painful, but I can't change it. I'll never see her again.

He remembered her warm body next to his, and the way she whispered his name. There must be another reason. She loves me, I know she does. She'll come to see me when she gets my letter.

I wish Jane could meet her.

Outside, night had fallen, and the birds had stopped singing. Alan Cole lay quietly on his bed, the tears running slowly down his face.

• • •

Jane sat on the chair in her flat and listened to the man and woman arguing in her kitchen. She could hear, but she couldn't speak or see, because the man had put a bag over her head. Her arms and legs were still tied to the chair, and her face ached where the man had hit her.

She tried to get her hands free. She pulled as hard as she could, but the rope just burned her wrists. All she could do was listen to the voices in the kitchen.

'We must phone him *now*, Kev. We can't wait.'

'We've got to wait. It's too dangerous to do it from here, Anna. Wait until we're ready to go.'

*Anna!* Jane thought. Was this her father's Anna? No, no, lots of women were called Anna.

'But we can't go until tonight,' Anna said. 'There are too many people around during the day. And every minute is important! Perhaps Cole has already talked to the police about me. Oh God, I wish the bomb had killed him with the others!'

'Well, it didn't. And it didn't kill the Queen.'

Jane's body was shaking. This *was* her father's Anna! She was talking about her father, and the bomb. And then Jane remembered where she had seen the woman before.

Outside Parliament, with a camera, shaking it angrily. Taking photos of the back of people's heads. Then pushing forwards to get closer, pressing the camera button again . . . a second before the bomb exploded.

The voices in the kitchen stopped. The door opened,

someone came into the room. *What now?*

Jane heard the click of a gun.

• • •

'Phone call for you, Mr Cole. You're popular today, aren't you?' The nurse smiled, pushed the telephone table next to his bed, and went out.

Alan picked up the phone. 'Hello?'

'Mr Cole? This is Detective David Hall. You remember I came to see you yesterday. I'm ringing because I've got a few more questions to ask you. Is it all right if I come over to see you now?'

'Er . . . well, I suppose so. But I've told you everything I know.'

'Yes, I'm sure. But it's just that we have to get all the facts right. I'll come over now, if that's OK?'

'Yes, fine. I . . .'

'Great! See you in a few minutes, then.'

Alan put the phone down slowly. He felt old, and tired, and very, very lonely. Perhaps I'll ring Jane later when this man's gone, he thought. I hope she remembered to post the letter.

• • •

Kev pulled the bag off Jane's head and she saw the gun a few centimetres from her eyes. 'I'm going to untie this cloth round your mouth,' Kev said. 'If you scream, I'll put a bullet through your head. This gun is silenced, no one will hear anything.'

They untied the cloth and pulled her chair over to the

wall, where the phone was. The gun was pointing at her head all the time.

'Do just what we tell you,' Anna said. 'And everything will be all right.'

Jane was suddenly wild with anger. She said: 'You're Anna, aren't you? My father loves you – he thinks you're wonderful. But you don't care about him at all, do you? You wish the bomb had killed him.'

'Of course I care about him,' Anna said softly. 'He's very important to me. That's why I'm going to phone him now, and you're going to talk to him too.'

Jane stared at her, then at Kev. 'Why?'

Anna laughed. 'I'm going to ask him to keep our love a secret. I have a very difficult husband, you know.'

What's the woman talking about? Jane thought. What does all this mean? Then, suddenly, a lot of things came together in her mind, and everything became clear. Anna had been with her father in the Mews on the night before the bombing. In the kitchen Anna had spoken about her father talking to the *police*. Jane could hear from Kev's voice that he was Irish, and he and Anna had moved out of Bowater Gardens on the morning of the bombing. Later, Anna had been outside Parliament, doing strange things with a camera when the bomb exploded. If it *was* a camera. Perhaps it had been a radio, sending a signal to the bomb. *Oh God!*

'You're the terrorists, aren't you?' she whispered. '*You* did it, Anna. *You* put the bomb in the Queen's coach. You exploded it with a camera. I saw you, outside Parliament.

You're terrorists – murdering terrorists, both of you!'

Kev smiled coldly. 'Well, well. What a clever little girl! But you're wrong. The police have arrested the terrorists. It was in the newspapers this morning.'

*'You're the terrorists, aren't you?' Jane whispered.*

'So? They're the wrong men, aren't they? It was you two, I know it was! You killed five people, and took away my father's leg, and now two innocent men will go to prison for thirty years, for something *you* did. But you don't care.'

Kev's eyes were suddenly full of hate. 'Care? About what? We're fighting to free Ireland. If the British put the wrong people in prison, that's not our problem. We care about staying free. That's good for Ireland.'

'Yes, and I suppose it's good for Ireland to use innocent people like my father – to make love to him just because you wanted to get into the Mews to put the bomb in the coach. Did you enjoy that, Anna? Do you feel proud of it?'

Anna laughed, a strange, quiet, cruel laugh. 'Yes, of course I enjoyed it, little girl. And your father enjoyed it too. I made him happy.'

'Happy!' Jane said. 'You nearly killed him!'

'Yes. I'm sorry he didn't die, while he was so happy.'

Silence. There was no answer to that, Jane thought.

'Let's get on with it,' said Kev angrily. 'We're losing time.'

Tears came into Jane's eyes. 'You dirty murderers,' she whispered.

Kev hit her across the face with his gun. Jane felt blood in her mouth. One of her teeth was broken.

'We could kill her now,' Kev said, 'and get out of the country tonight.'

'No, no,' Anna said. 'We must talk to Cole first.'

'But we can't let her go,' Kev said. 'She's seen our faces. She knows too much.'

'Oh no,' Anna said. Her voice was soft and cruel. 'Of course not. But we'll keep her alive for some weeks, to make sure that Cole stays quiet. Pick up the phone, Kev.'

# 4

## Phone call

The phone rang again in Alan Cole's room.

'Hello?' he said.

'Alan?'

He recognized her voice at once. 'Anna!' he said, his heart beating fast.

'Yes. Now listen carefully, Alan—'

'Oh Anna! I've been waiting for your call. Have you heard about – about my leg, Anna?'

'Never mind your leg. Listen to me. I'll say this once and once only.'

'What? Anna, what are you—'

'We've got your daughter, Alan. Jane. That's her name, isn't it? Speak to your father, Jane. *Now!*'

Over the phone, Alan heard the high, frightened voice of his daughter. 'Dad? I'm sorry, Dad. They say if you tell the police anything about Anna, they'll kill me, but I don't care, I . . . oh!'

Alan heard a scream, which was suddenly cut off. Then Anna's voice again: 'She won't die if you keep quiet, lover boy. But if you say a word, a single word about me to the police, you'll find her body in the river Thames. Do you understand?'

Alan tried to speak, but there was something wrong with his voice. 'Yes,' he said. 'But, please . . .'

'No buts. If you want to see your daughter again, keep your mouth *shut*.'

The phone went dead. Alan Cole sat very still. There was a terrible pain in his chest, his mouth was dry and he couldn't move. He sat like a stone.

It's like a dream, he thought. Surely it didn't happen. But that voice on the phone, it was Jane all right. And Anna, too. *Anna!* . . . saying that she had kidnapped Jane.

But why? What was going on?

Slowly, he tried to understand. He hadn't told the police about Anna, because of her husband. But why was that so important?

*Why has Anna kidnapped Jane?*

Because Anna has a secret. Something very important that I, Alan, know about, but mustn't tell the police. Anna will kill Jane if I tell anyone about it.

But what is this secret! What am I supposed to know?

There was a knock on the door. A nurse came in.

'Hello, Mr Cole. A policeman to see you. Are you OK?'

'Yes . . . yes, fine thanks.'

'You don't look OK.' The nurse put her hand on his head, and felt his wrist. 'Well, you're not too hot, and your heart's OK.' She smiled at the policeman. 'Just half an hour, now. Remember, he's had a very serious accident.'

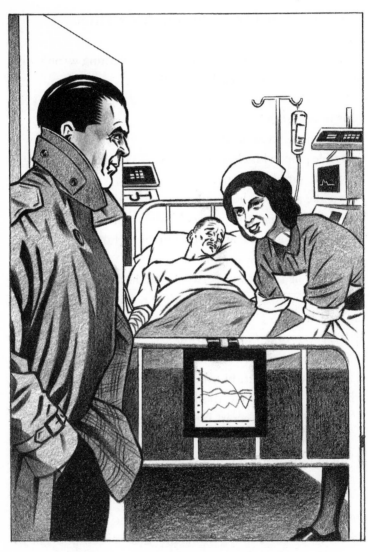

'*Remember, he's had a very serious accident.*'

'I know that.' The policeman came in and sat down, and the nurse went out, pushing the telephone table in front of her. 'I'm Detective Hall, Mr Cole. We met before.'

'Yes,' Alan said. The policeman had a kind, friendly face. The kind of man you could trust. He'll help me, Alan thought. He's probably a father himself.

*No!* Fear burned Alan like a fire. *I mustn't tell him about Anna. If I do, Jane will die . . .*

'You've probably read in the newspapers, Mr Cole, that we've arrested two men.' The policeman told Alan the story about the two Irishmen in the coach factory. 'So we know they bombed the coach, and how they did it. I suppose you're pleased about that.'

'Er . . . yes,' Alan said quietly. 'That's good. But . . . why have you come to see me?'

'I just need to ask you a few questions about the day before the bombing. You see, we think these men put the bomb in the coach three days before the bombing, while the coach was at the factory. So the bomb was already in the coach when it came back to the Mews.'

'Was it?' Alan said. He didn't really understand what the policeman was talking about.

'We think so, yes. And in your job, you look after the coach, don't you?'

'The coach, yes. And the horses. Mostly the horses.'

'Well, did you notice anything unusual – anything at all?'

'No, I don't think so.'

'Let's take this slowly,' the policeman said. 'The day before

33

the bombing, when did you leave work?'

'At . . . about six o'clock. Half past, perhaps.'

'And you didn't go back?'

'No,' Alan said quietly.

Then he looked away, quickly, out of the window. He felt cold, frightened, lonely.

'Are you sure about that, Mr Cole? You see, a guard told me you came back later, at about ten.'

'He did? Oh, yes, of course. I went back to see a horse, Sandman. He had a bad leg.'

'I see.' The policeman wrote in his book. 'Alone?'

'I'm sorry?'

'Were you alone, Mr Cole? When you saw the horse?'

For a moment Alan didn't answer. A new, very unwelcome idea came to him, and he began to feel sick with fear. *It wasn't those two Irishmen*, he thought, *it was Anna!* She put the bomb in the coach when I was with Sandman. I was alone with the horse for at least ten minutes; she had plenty of time.

And that means she didn't love me at all, she just used me. I thought I was so lucky, an old man with a young pretty woman in my bed – and all the time she was laughing at me. Worse than that – she's a murderer! She killed George and Bernard and John, and she took my leg, and now she's going to kill Jane as well!

And I can't say anything about it.

That's why she phoned me. To make sure that I never tell the police.

*If I tell this policeman, Jane will die.*

In a strange, shaky voice, Alan said: 'I was alone when I was with the horse, yes.'

The policeman said nothing. Alan felt his hands shaking and put them under the sheet. Why is he looking at me like that? he thought. What does he know?

'Are you sure, Mr Cole? The guard says you have a lady friend, and sometimes she visits the horses with you. Was she with you that night?'

'No.'

'You're sure about that, Mr Cole?'

'Yes, I am. And she's not my friend any more now – we've ended it.'

'I see.' The policeman sighed, wrote in his notebook, and stood up. 'That's all then, Mr Cole. The guard wasn't sure. Probably it was a different night.'

'Yes. I'm sure it was.'

'Right then. Thank you for your help. Goodnight, Mr Cole.' He walked to the door, and went out.

Alan watched him go, unable to say another word. He had never felt so helpless, so frightened. I have to speak, he thought, I have to do something. But I can't.

If I speak, Jane will die.

But if I say nothing, will they ever let her go?

As the door closed, he opened his mouth and said: 'Detective Hall.'

But the policeman walked away. He didn't hear.

Oh God, Alan thought. *What do I do now?*

• • •

After the phone call Kev and Anna tied the cloth round Jane's mouth again, and went back into her kitchen. She had the bag over her head too, but she could hear most of what they were saying. They were angry, arguing.

'You've made too many mistakes with this plan, Anna,'

*Jane could hear what they were saying.*

Kev said. 'The Queen of England is still walking around Buckingham Palace because of you.'

Anna's voice was high and angry. 'Because of *me*? What about *you*? You're supposed to understand bombs and radio transmitters, and what happens? The transmitter in that camera didn't work when I pressed the button!'

'You probably didn't press it hard enough,' Kev said coldly. 'It worked in the end, didn't it?'

'Yes, too late!' Anna said. 'That was *your* mistake, not mine. So now we've got Cole to worry about, and this girl. We've got to get her away from here fast.'

'Wait until midnight, when the house is quiet.'

There was an icy fear in Jane's stomach. They know I can hear them, and they don't care, she thought. I'm sure Dad will keep quiet, but they can never let me go now. They'll have to kill me, because I know too much.

If I don't get away from them soon, I'm going to die.

• • •

Alan lay in the dark and listened to the voices in his head, arguing this way, and that way, until he thought he would go crazy.

*Keep your mouth shut! If you speak, she'll die.*

But they'll still kill her, if she's seen their faces.

*They won't, Anna won't. She's a woman, she couldn't do that! She was your lover!*

Woman! She killed five people! She blew my leg off!

*Those two men the police have arrested are innocent. They'll go to prison for thirty years if I don't speak!*

37

I don't know them, I don't care about them. Jane is the only person who matters to me!

*The police will think that I helped Anna put the bomb in the coach! I'll go to prison.*

That woman is laughing at me. She was laughing at me when we made love. I hate her! I hope she dies!

*She won't die, Jane will. I must keep quiet!*

What can I do? If I speak, they'll kill her. But if I don't speak, they'll kill her later. So I've got to tell the police now, it's Jane's only chance.

*I can't, it's too dangerous. I can't! I want to see my daughter!*

For two hours he lay in his room and listened to the voices in his head and thought he was going crazy. His leg ached, his chest felt very hot. Twice he decided to get up and tell someone, but his body wouldn't move.

Then, the third time, he got into his wheelchair and went out into the corridor. It was midnight.

'Nurse!' he said. 'Nurse, I need a telephone, now!'

Oh God, he thought. *Where is Jane now?*

• • •

Jane was in the boot of a car. Her hands and feet were tied, the piece of cloth was round her mouth, and the bag was over her head, but she knew she was in a car boot because she could hear the engine, and when she tried to sit up she hit her head.

She didn't know how long she had been there. There wasn't much air, but she couldn't do anything about it. She just lay there and thought: it can't be much longer. We must get there soon and then they'll let me out.

And then what? How long before they kill me?

## 5

## 'You must believe me!'

When Alan phoned the police, Detective Hall came to the hospital quickly, bringing an Inspector Lee with him. They listened to Alan's story, then talked for a while outside the door. Then they came back in.

'OK, Mr Cole,' Inspector Lee said. 'Detectives are now searching the house in Bowater Gardens and your daughter's flat. I've informed the police at ports and airports too. It's possible that the kidnappers will try to take your daughter out of the country, you know.'

'Oh my God.' Alan held his face in his hands. 'She's probably dead. I'll never see her again.'

'Let's hope that's not true,' said the Inspector. 'Now, let's talk about this woman Anna again. Why do you think she's a terrorist?'

Again, Alan explained. The visit to the Mews the evening before the bombing; the ten minutes when Anna was not with him; her phone call, telling him not to talk to the police or Jane would die. It was hard to speak clearly because he was so angry and afraid. He began to cry. 'It's no good,' he said. 'Jane's going to die.'

39

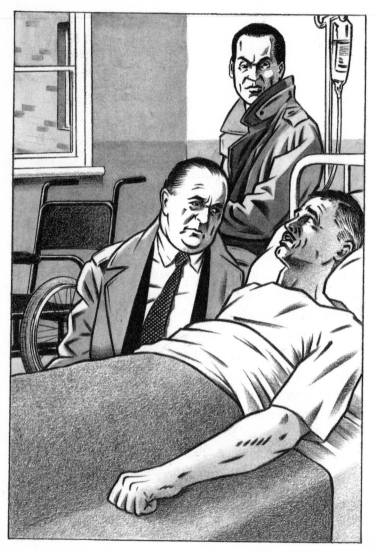

'It's no good,' Alan said. 'Jane's going to die.'

'Try to keep calm, Mr Cole,' said the Inspector. 'You see, we're not sure that this Anna *is* a terrorist. We have already arrested the two men who put the bomb in the coach. In fact, one of them confessed to it this morning. The other one will confess soon.'

'But they're the wrong people – they must be! If *they* are the murderers, why did Anna phone me? Why is she saying she'll kill my daughter if I don't keep quiet about *her*?'

'Are you sure it was Anna's voice on the phone?'

'Of course I am! And it was Jane's voice as well! I know my own daughter's voice, don't I?' Alan shouted.

'Mmm,' the Inspector said slowly. 'Now, your daughter. Was she unhappy to hear about Anna, do you think? Sometimes daughters don't like their fathers to have girlfriends, you know. Perhaps she was angry with you.'

'No. Not really. Well, perhaps a bit.'

'I see some very strange things in my job, Mr Cole, and a lot of them are because of family arguments. It's just possible, you see, that your daughter hasn't been kidnapped at all. Perhaps she's angry with you and wants to stop you seeing Anna. Perhaps – I've seen it happen before – she's asked a friend to ring you and pretend to be Anna . . .'

'No!' Alan shouted. 'Jane isn't like that! She was frightened, I could hear it in her voice on the phone. ANNA HAS KIDNAPPED HER! You must believe me!'

At that moment another detective came in and spoke quietly to Inspector Lee, who immediately got up and left the room. When he came back, his face was serious.

'The house in Bowater Gardens is empty,' he told Alan. 'The two people there left on the morning of the bombing. We didn't find anything useful at your daughter's flat – but we did find her handbag with her flat keys in it. It seems strange for her to go out without her keys, doesn't it?'

'Where is she?' Alan whispered. 'Can you find her?'

'If your daughter has been kidnapped, she could be anywhere,' the Inspector said. 'Our only hope is that the kidnappers call you again, and then we can find out where the call came from. We're fixing up a phone for you now, and there'll be two policewomen here with you all night. If Anna does phone, keep her talking. Tell her that you have said nothing to the police, and ask to speak to Jane. Say you must hear her voice.'

They put the phone on a table next to Alan's bed. He stared at it, saying to himself over and over again:

*I must hear her voice. I must hear her voice.*

• • •

They put Jane in a small bedroom, untied her feet, and took the bag off her head. But they tied her hands behind her back, and then tied them to the end of the bed.

'You'll stay here until those two men are sent to prison,' Anna said. 'Every day we'll send your father a picture of you with today's newspaper, to show you're still alive.'

'Then what?'

'Then . . . we'll see. Perhaps, if your father is a good boy, we'll let you go,' Anna said. 'If you keep quiet too.'

But Jane was watching Kev's face. He won't let me go, she

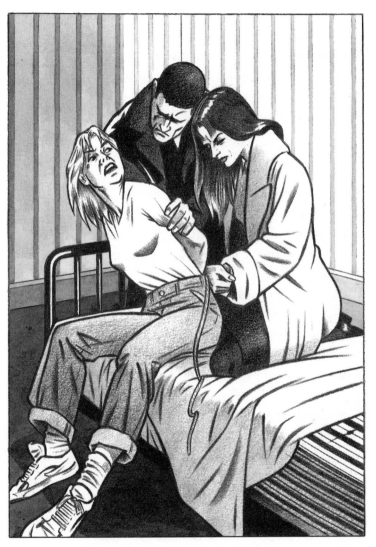

*They tied her hands behind her back.*

thought. Never. If I don't escape, I'll die here.

When they had left the room, she lay in the dark, wondering how she could escape. I don't want to die, she thought. And how terrible it will be for Dad if they kill me. And then there are those two innocent Irishmen, who will spend thirty years in prison for something they didn't do.

That bastard Kev's going to kill me. I've got to try to escape. I just have to.

For hours she tried to get free but it was impossible. The rope only hurt her wrists more. But at least she could move her hands, up and down the end of the old bed. Once, towards morning, she pulled the rope hard against the bed, but it didn't break. Instead, something cut her hand, and she had an idea.

Could it cut the rope as well?

She moved the rope up and down across the end of the bed. It was very difficult because she couldn't see what she was doing. Three times she cut herself, and there was blood on the rope. But by early morning, the rope broke. Her hands were free! What now?

She tried the door but it was locked. Downstairs, she could hear a radio, and she could smell coffee. So one of them, at least, was in the house.

Then she had another idea. She lay down on the bed and arranged the rope around her wrists, behind her back. Then she screamed: 'Hey! You! Terrorist murderers! Come up here now! I'm thirsty! Get up here and give me a drink!'

In a few minutes, she heard someone on the stairs.

• • •

'Breakfast, Mr Cole,' the nurse said. 'Eat up like a good boy, then you'll feel better.' She smiled.

I'm not a child, Alan thought. Oh God, I'm a father who's lost a child! He pushed the eggs and tomatoes away, and drank a cup of black coffee.

The policewoman in the armchair woke up and smiled brightly. 'Well, no one has phoned, Mr Cole. Perhaps your daughter has been to an all-night party and she'll be along to see you this morning.'

Alan stared at her hopelessly. He had not closed his eyes all night. So the police didn't really believe him. Perhaps they thought he had gone crazy because he had lost a leg. He stared at the silent phone.

*Ring, damn you! Ring!*

• • •

Kev came in, carrying his cup of coffee in his hand. He wasn't wearing a coat, so Jane could see the gun under his arm. 'Stop making that noise,' he said. 'Or you'll be sorry.'

Jane looked at him. 'You stupid little man,' she said softly, and as Kev stepped angrily forwards, she freed her hands from the rope behind her back and jumped at him. With one hand she pulled his head down, and with the other she grabbed his cup and threw the hot coffee into his face. Then she kicked him hard in the stomach.

'Aaaah! Damn you . . .' Kev fell onto the floor, trying to get the hot coffee out of his eyes. Immediately Jane jumped on top of him. Her knees landed hard in his stomach, and her

45

*She pulled his head down, and threw the hot coffee into his face.*

fingers tried to get the gun under his arm. But Kev's hand found the gun first. Jane tried to pull it out of his hand, but he was too strong for her. With his other hand he hit her hard on the side of the head.

Jane fell forwards. But as she fell, she put her head down and bit his nose until her mouth was full of blood. He screamed, tried to pull his head away . . .

And let go of the gun.

I've got it, Jane thought. I've really got it! Then Kev hit her head again, hard, and she didn't know what was happening. She moved away from him, bringing the gun down towards her chest. Her head hurt terribly, and there was blood in her mouth, but all the time her fingers were trying to use the gun.

Why won't it shoot? she thought. How do I make it work? Then as Kev hit her again, there was a BANG and another BANG and a third and a fourth. She didn't know what the bangs were but she held on to the gun as hard as she could and there was a fifth BANG and a sixth . . .

And then it stopped. She opened her eyes and saw that Kev wasn't hitting her any more. His hands had gone all soft and there was blood coming out of his face and his neck and his chest, there was blood all over the floor and half of his head was missing.

Jane stood up, shaking. Where is Anna? she thought.

# 6

# In the tunnel

Alan put down his coffee when the call came. He picked up the phone with shaking hands. A voice said: 'Alan?'

'Anna,' Alan whispered. The policewoman went out of

47

the door and spoke in a low voice on her radio.

'Do you remember what I said yesterday, Alan?'

'Yes,' Alan said. 'Please don't hurt Jane. Please. I haven't said a word to anyone. I promise you, Anna.'

'Good. Not today, not tomorrow, not ever, Alan. Do you understand? Not if you want her to stay alive.'

'Yes, I understand, Anna. But I must speak to Jane. I must hear her voice, Anna. How do I know you haven't killed her already?' Alan's voice was shaking.

Anna laughed, gently, cruelly. 'We'll send you something, Alan. In a day or two. If you're good.'

'Anna, *please*.'

But the phone went dead.

Alan put the phone down slowly, and suddenly the room was full of voices.

'We've got it! A phone box in South Kensington station, by the ticket office . . .'

'Calling all cars in Kensington, calling all cars in Kensington. A woman has just made a phone call from . . .'

The policewoman put her hand on Alan's arm. 'They'll be there in two minutes,' she said gently. 'They'll—'

'Take me there!' Alan said. 'Please!'

The policewoman looked at him, then at the wheelchair, then back at Alan's white face. 'All right. We've got a big van outside. We can get the wheelchair in that.'

•  •  •

As Jane came down the stairs, she realized two things; she was covered in blood, and Anna wasn't there.

The house was very quiet, and all the rooms were empty. But I can't go out all covered in blood, she thought. People will think I've killed someone.

*I have.* But I had to, he was going to kill me. And he's a terrorist. He killed five people, he and Anna . . . I must get out before Anna comes back.

She found a man's coat, put it on, and went out into the street. I should call a policeman, she thought. But she could only see ordinary people, women and children. She saw an underground station and walked towards it.

She went into the station, found some money in the coat pocket, and bought a ticket. I must find my father, she thought, and tell him that everything's all right. Then she looked behind her and saw a woman coming out of a telephone box.

Oh my God, she thought, it's *Anna!*

Jane walked quickly away from the ticket office, down the escalator towards the platform and the trains. Halfway down the escalator she looked back up behind her.

Anna had seen her! She was following her down the escalator!

Quickly, Jane ran down to the bottom and onto one of the platforms. There was a train there, with its doors still open. She ran towards them, but as she ran, the doors closed and the train moved away into the tunnel. Anna was now coming onto the platform behind her. Anna's hand was inside her coat and Jane was sure she had a gun.

Why didn't I bring Kev's gun? Jane thought. But it was

*Anna was following her down the escalator!*

empty and I hate guns and it's no use thinking about that now. *What do I do now?*

• • •

As the police van screamed through the London traffic, the policewoman listened in to her radio and passed the information to Alan.

'Inspector Lee is on his way,' she said. 'There are six cars at the station already and they're watching all the entrances. Ah! Two detectives have seen a woman with red-brown hair going down the escalator . . .'

'But the trains,' Alan said. 'She'll catch a train . . .'

'They'll stop the trains as soon as they can. But there are hundreds of people in the station. The detectives could lose the woman in the crowds . . .'

'Please God,' whispered Alan. 'Let them catch her.'

• • •

As Anna came towards her, Jane ran towards the end of the platform, then looked behind her and saw Anna running after her, her hand still inside her coat. Quickly, Jane turned and ran towards another escalator, but there was a crowd of people there. She looked again and saw Anna twenty metres behind. She turned round a corner, back onto another platform which was empty – no people, no train. Anna will find me here in a second and shoot me, she thought. *What now?*

She jumped off the platform onto the railway line, and ran into the tunnel.

It was very dark in the tunnel. She knew that one of the

lines was electric. If I touch it, I'll die, she thought. The trains come every six minutes, and if a train hits me, I'll die too. And there are only thirty centimetres between the sides of the train and the tunnel walls.

But there are holes in the tunnel walls every hundred metres, for workmen. I'll find one of those, wait for the next train and then go on to the next hole. It's probably only a kilometre to the next station. And perhaps Anna won't be sure which way I've gone.

She ran on into the darkness. Once she fell, and her hands nearly touched the electric line. When she got up, there was a terrible noise, like a train coming. But it was a train in another tunnel, not this one. She ran on, with one hand on the wall, looking for the hole.

Three minutes, four . . . then she found it! A hole just big enough for one person. She got in and stood very still, waiting. She heard the terrible noise again, this time from the station behind her. Then it stopped. The train will stop in that station for one minute, she thought. Then it will come past.

She laughed aloud in the darkness. Anna is still looking for me back on the platform. How angry she must be!

*A hand touched her arm.* She screamed. 'What? *Oh God, no!*' The hand grabbed her arm, and pulled her out of the hole, into the dark tunnel.

'Get out there!'

Two hands pushed her and Jane fell between the lines. She got to her knees, carefully, afraid of the electric line. Then

the terrible noise started. The ground shook beneath her
feet and a white light came towards her, faster and faster. In
the light Jane saw Anna standing in the hole, with a gun in
her hand. She jumped towards the hole but the train was

*Jane saw Anna standing in the hole, with a gun in her hand.*

53

coming faster, much too fast, and there was only room in the hole for one person, a woman with a gun . . .

· · ·

When Alan arrived at the station, there were police cars everywhere, and crowds of people watching them. The policewoman helped him out of the van and he pushed his wheelchair through the crowd, shouting angrily, 'What's happening? Where is she?'

At the top of the escalator a policeman said: 'I'm sorry, sir. You can't go down. There's been a terrible accident.'

Then some ambulance men arrived. 'Where is it?' they asked.

'Down in the tunnel. Two women – a train's hit them,' the policeman said. The ambulance men hurried down.

'What's happening?' Alan shouted. 'Which women? There's a murderer down there, a terrorist! And my daughter – I've got to find my daughter!'

He began to climb out of his wheelchair, but the policeman pushed him back. 'I'm sorry, sir.'

Then the policewoman hurried up and explained. They helped Alan's wheelchair onto the escalator and went down. At the bottom Alan saw an empty train, and a lot of police at the end of the platform. The ambulance men talked to the police, and then went into the tunnel. Alan wheeled his chair slowly along the platform.

Then two of the ambulance men came out of the tunnel. There was a young woman between them. She walked slowly, she was very dirty, and there was blood on the side of her face. But Alan knew who she was.

'Jane,' he said. '*Jane!* Are you all right?'

Jane looked along the platform and saw him. '*Dad?* Why

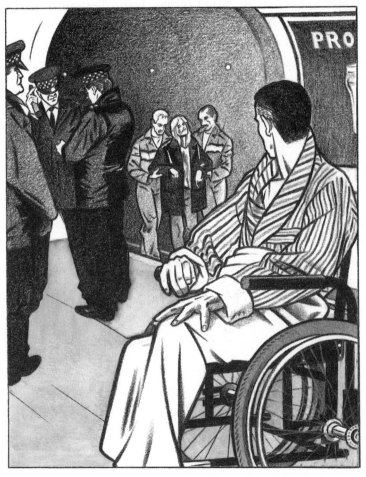

*Alan knew who she was.*

55

are you here?' She walked towards him shakily.

'I came to find you,' Alan said. 'Oh God, Jane, what happened? Did Anna try to kill you?'

Jane touched the blood on her face. 'Yes. She tried to shoot me but she missed. Then I threw her in front of a train. I killed the other one, too.' She smiled, a strange, shaky smile. 'You said there was no justice in this life, didn't you, Dad? Well, those two terrorists murdered five people, and took away your leg and . . . and now they're dead! So there is *some* justice, Dad, isn't there?' Then her eyes filled with tears, and she sat down, suddenly, on a platform seat. 'That woman hated you, Dad,' she whispered shakily, 'really hated you.'

Alan wheeled his chair close to her and held her hands in his. 'I'm so sorry,' he said. 'Anna hated everyone, not just me. But she doesn't matter now, Jane. You're alive! That's all that matters to me. That's all that matters in the world.'

# GLOSSARY

**artificial**  not natural; made by people
**bastard** *(slang)*  a bad or cruel person (usually a man)
**bloody**  bleeding or covered in blood; also, a word used to show that you are angry
**boot**  the place at the back of a car for luggage
**chest**  the top front part of your body
**click**  a short sharp sound
**coach**  a kind of 'car' pulled by horses
**confess**  to say that you have done something wrong
**cruel**  not kind; bringing pain or trouble to other people
**damn**  a word that shows you are angry
**doll**  a children's toy that looks like a person
**electric**  using electricity (power that can make light, heat, etc.)
**embarrassed**  feeling uncomfortable or ashamed about what other people will think
**escalator**  stairs that can move and carry people up and down
**expect**  to think or believe that something will happen
**God (my God!)**  words you say when you are very surprised
**grab**  to take hold of something quickly and violently
**guard** *(n)*  someone who watches and keeps a building safe
**hell (who the hell?)**  a question showing you are surprised or angry
**hesitate**  to stop for a moment, showing that you are not sure about what you are doing or saying
**human**  a person, not an animal
**innocent**  not having done wrong
**judo**  a kind of fighting sport
**justice**  when bad people are punished and good people are saved
**kick** *(v)*  to hit something or someone with the foot

**kidnap**   to take somebody prisoner in order to get money or other things from their family

**kiss** *(v)*   to touch someone lovingly with your lips

**look after**   to take care of

**make love**   to have sex

**mews**   a building (in a town) for horses

**ordinary**   usual; not special or different in any way

**parliament**   the building where a country's laws are made

**platform**   the part of a station where you get on and off trains

**port**   a town or city next to the sea where boats stop

**proud**   feeling pleased about something you have done

**queen**   the most important lady in a country

**rope**   very thick, strong string

**shoulder**   the part of your body between your neck and your arm

**sigh** *(v)*   to breathe out slowly when you are sad, tired, etc.

**signal** *(n)*   a message without words, using sounds, flags, radio, etc.

**stare** *(v)*   to look very hard at something for a long time

**stroke** *(v)*   to move your hand slowly and gently over something

**tears**   water that comes from the eyes when you cry

**terrorist**   someone who uses violence (kidnapping, bombing, etc.) to get what they want

**throw** (past tense **threw**)   to move your arm quickly to send something through the air

**tie** *(v)*   to fasten two things together with rope

**transmitter**   the part of a radio that sends signals

**trust** *(v)*   to believe that someone is good, honest, etc.

**tunnel**   a long hole underground, e.g. for trains

**underground**   below the ground; also, the underground railway

**van**   a kind of big car or small covered lorry for carrying things

# Justice

## ACTIVITIES

## *Before Reading*

1 **Read the back cover, and the story introduction on the first page of the book. They will give you the answers to six of the questions below. Find the questions, and answer them.**

   1 Where did the bombing happen?
   2 What was Alan Cole doing when the bomb went off?
   3 Why was Jane Cole in the crowd?
   4 Was the Queen hurt?
   5 How many people were hurt?
   6 How badly was Alan Cole hurt?
   7 Who were the five people who died?
   8 Which country were the terrorists from?
   9 What hasn't Alan realized yet?

   **You will find the other three answers in Chapter 1.**

2 **Can you guess how the story ends? Choose one of these ideas. Which ending would be the best justice? Why?**

   1 The terrorists are caught and sent to prison.
   2 The terrorists are shot by the police during a chase.
   3 Jane Cole kills the terrorists.
   4 Alan Cole kills one of the terrorists.
   5 The terrorists kill Jane Cole.
   6 Another bomb explodes and kills Alan Cole.
   7 Nobody ever catches the terrorists.

# *While Reading*

**Read Chapter 1. Answer the other three questions from Activity 1 in *Before Reading*, and then look at these sentences. Are they true (T) or false (F)? Change the false sentences into true ones.**

1 At the moment when the bomb exploded, Jane was saying something to the American tourists.
2 Jane was badly hurt while helping to save her father.
3 Jane cared more about her father than anyone else in the world.
4 The doctors were unable to save Alan's leg.
5 Alan will probably ride, swim, and climb again.
6 Alan heard about his dead friends, and was very angry.

**Read Chapter 2, and then answer these questions.**

1 Why did the police arrest the two Irishmen?
2 Why was Alan in the Mews the night before the bombing?
3 How long had Alan known Anna?
4 How did Jane feel about her father's new woman friend?
5 Why had Alan written a letter to Anna?
6 Why did Jane decide to take the letter, not post it?
7 What did Jane find out at 14 Bowater Gardens?
8 What did Jane think when she first saw the woman in her flat?
9 Why did Jane stop fighting?

**Before you read Chapter 3, can you guess what the man and the woman do next? Choose one of these ideas.**

1 They steal the valuables from Jane's flat and then go away.
2 They kidnap Jane and take her out of the country.
3 They keep her prisoner in a house somewhere in London.
4 They kill her.

**Read Chapters 3 and 4. Complete these sentences with the right names.**

1 _____ soon realized who _____ and _____ were.
2 _____ wanted to kill _____ and get out of the country that night, but _____ wanted to talk to _____ first.
3 When _____ picked up the phone, he heard first _____'s voice, then _____'s voice, and then a scream from _____.
4 _____ realized that _____ had put the bomb in the coach, but he was afraid to say anything because of _____.

**Now match these halves of sentences. Who said these words? To whom? When?**

1 'If you scream, . . .
2 'If you say a single word about me to the police, . . .
3 'If I don't get away from them soon, . . .
4 'If I speak, . . .
5 . . . you'll find her body in the river Thames.'
6 . . . they'll kill her.'
7 . . . I'll put a bullet through your head.'
8 . . . I'm going to die.'

**Before you read Chapter 5, can you answer this question?**

The chapter title is '*You must believe me!*' Who do you think
will say this, to whom?

**Read Chapter 5. Match each question-word to a question, and
then answer the questions.**

*How / What / Where / Who / Why*

1  . . . didn't the police think that Anna was a terrorist?
2  . . . did the police find Jane's handbag and flat keys?
3  . . . did Jane free herself from the bed?
4  . . . did Jane do with Kev's cup of hot coffee?
5  . . . killed Kev with his own gun?

**Before you read Chapter 6, can you guess what happens next?
Choose Y (yes) or N (no) for each of these ideas.**

1  Anna comes running upstairs with a gun. Y/N
2  Jane leaves the house and goes to the hospital. Y/N
3  Jane meets Anna in an underground station. Y/N
4  Anna goes to the hospital and tries to shoot Alan. Y/N

**Read Chapter 6, and complete these sentences in your own
words.**

1  The police discovered where Anna was when _____.
2  Halfway down the escalator, Jane _____.
3  Jane hid in a hole in the tunnel wall, but _____.
4  When the train came towards Jane, she _____.
5  All that mattered to Alan was that _____.

## *After Reading*

**1 Use the clues to complete this crossword with words from the story.**

1 To touch lovingly with your lips.

2 Terrorists kill people with these.

3 A kind of fighting sport.

4 To believe someone is honest.

5 Alan wrote this, to Anna.

6 A telephone does this.

7 Very unkind.

8 Jane lived in one of these.

9 To hit with your foot.

10 To murder.

11 Jane was tied up with this.

12 An animal that pulls a coach.

13 The opposite of love.

14 To take hold of violently.

**Now you should find a sentence of four words, reading down the dark boxes.**

1 What is the sentence?

2 Who said this to Jane, and where?

3 What did Jane think that the person was doing at the time?

4 What was the person really doing?

5 What happened next?

2 **Look at these sentences. Which advice would Jane choose, do you think? Which would *you* choose? Why?**

1 If you are kidnapped, you should . . .
   a) pretend to be ill.   b) try to escape.   c) wait for help.

2 If the kidnappers speak to you, you should . . .
   a) not answer.   b) answer politely.   c) shout at them.

3 If the kidnappers tell you to do something, you should . . .
   a) do it at once.   b) refuse to do it.   c) argue about it.

4 If the kidnappers get angry with you, you should . . .
   a) stare at them.   b) look at the floor.   c) start to cry.

3 **What did Anna and Kev say to each other when they met after the bombing? Put their conversation in the right order, and write in the speakers' names. Begin with number 6.**

1 _____ 'In hospital. The radio said that he's lost a leg. But he'll start to wonder about you soon, won't he?'

2 _____ 'Yes, a student flat in north London.'

3 _____ 'Forget the transmitter. We've got a new problem. Cole isn't dead! The other three are, but not Cole.'

4 _____ 'No, he won't, Kev. He's in love with me.'

5 _____ 'Good! We kidnap her, and tell Cole to keep his mouth shut. Do you know where she lives?'

6 _____ 'Your stupid transmitter, Kev! It didn't work!'

7 _____ 'In love? Don't be stupid, Anna! The man's lost a leg. He'll put two and two together, and he'll talk.'

8 _____ 'Oh no! Why did it have to be him? Where is he?'

9 _____ 'Right, let's get moving, Anna!'

10 _____ 'So how do we stop him? Ah! His daughter Jane!'

4 **Here are some extracts from police telephone calls or radio messages. Choose one suitable word for each gap, and then put the extracts in the right order for the story.**

1 'Cole's changed his story. He now says that his girl friend is one of the _____ and that she's _____ his daughter. Send some men to _____ the woman's house and the daughter's _____. Got a pen? Here are the addresses . . .'

2 'We're in South Kensington _____. Just seen a woman with red-brown _____ going down the _____. She's in a great hurry. We're going after her . . .'

3 'Detective Hall has just been to see Cole again. Cole has repeated that he was _____ in the Mews that night. And he isn't seeing this woman any more.'

4 'We've just heard that a _____ has exploded outside _____ and has destroyed the Queen's _____. Get every man down there at once!'

5 'Inspector Lee? We're in Jane Cole's flat now, and we've just found her _____ with her flat _____ in it. It's a bit _____ for her to go out without them, isn't it, sir?'

6 'The _____ at the Mews thinks that Cole had his new _____ friend with him that night, but he isn't sure. Cole has said _____ about this woman. Let's talk to him again.'

7 'I'm at the hospital now. Alan Cole is the only _____ who is still _____, but I can't speak to him yet. His leg was very badly _____ and the doctors have had to cut it _____.'

5 **Perhaps Jane sent a quick email to her brother in Australia to tell him about the kidnap. Complete her email for her (use as many words as you like).**

A lot has happened since you phoned, Philip. When I went back to my flat, the two terrorists who _____. The woman was _____, who had put _____. They said that they _____ if Dad said _____. In the end I escaped, and both the terrorists _____. The man was killed by _____ and the woman was hit by _____. Must get back to Dad now. I'll tell you more later. Love, Jane.

6 **Do you agree (A) or disagree (D) with these ideas? Why?**

1 Jane was as much of a murderer as Anna and Kev.

2 It is always wrong to use violence to get what you want.

3 A 'terrorist' for one person can be a 'freedom fighter' for another person.

7 **Are some of these crimes more serious than others? Put them in order, 1 to 6, with number 1 for the most serious crime. How would you punish each person? Explain why.**

- A terrorist whose bomb kills five people and hurts forty.
- A bank robber who shoots dead an armed policeman.
- A drunk driver who kills a child in a road accident.
- A wife who buys a gun and kills her violent husband.
- A gunman who goes crazy and shoots ten people in a shop.
- A crazy gunman who shoots ten children in a school.

# ABOUT THE AUTHOR

Tim Vicary is an experienced teacher and writer, and has written several stories for the Oxford Bookworms Library. Many of these are in the Thriller & Adventure series, such as *Skyjack!* (at Stage 3), or in the True Stories series, such as *The Brontë Story* (also at Stage 3), which is about the lives of the famous novelists, Charlotte, Emily, and Anne Brontë.

Tim Vicary has two children, and keeps dogs, cats, and horses. He lives and works in York, in the north of England, and has also published two long novels, *The Blood upon the Rose* and *Cat and Mouse*.

# ABOUT BOOKWORMS

## OXFORD BOOKWORMS LIBRARY
*Classics • True Stories • Fantasy & Horror • Human Interest*
*Crime & Mystery • Thriller & Adventure*

The OXFORD BOOKWORMS LIBRARY offers a wide range of original and adapted stories, both classic and modern, which take learners from elementary to advanced level through six carefully graded language stages:

**Stage 1** (400 headwords)      **Stage 4** (1400 headwords)

**Stage 2** (700 headwords)      **Stage 5** (1800 headwords)

**Stage 3** (1000 headwords)     **Stage 6** (2500 headwords)

More than fifty titles are also available on cassette, and there are many titles at Stages 1 to 4 which are specially recommended for younger learners. In addition to the introductions and activities in each Bookworm, resource material includes photocopiable test worksheets and Teacher's Handbooks, which contain advice on running a class library and using cassettes, and the answers for the activities in the books.

---

Several other series are linked to the OXFORD BOOKWORMS LIBRARY. They range from highly illustrated readers for young learners, to playscripts, non-fiction readers, and unsimplified texts for advanced learners.

*Oxford Bookworms Starters*        *Oxford Bookworms Factfiles*
*Oxford Bookworms Playscripts*     *Oxford Bookworms Collection*

Details of these series and a full list of all titles in the OXFORD BOOKWORMS LIBRARY can be found in the *Oxford English* catalogues. A selection of titles from the OXFORD BOOKWORMS LIBRARY can be found on the next pages.

BOOKWORMS • CRIME & MYSTERY • STAGE 3

# The Last Sherlock Holmes Story

## MICHAEL DIBDIN

### Retold by Rosalie Kerr

For fifty years after Dr Watson's death, a packet of papers, written by the doctor himself, lay hidden in a locked box. The papers contained an extraordinary report of the case of Jack the Ripper and the horrible murders in the East End of London in 1888. The detective, of course, was the great Sherlock Holmes – but why was the report kept hidden for so long?

This is the story that Sir Arthur Conan Doyle never wrote. It is a strange and frightening tale . . .

BOOKWORMS • THRILLER & ADVENTURE • STAGE 3

# Chemical Secret

## TIM VICARY

The job was too good. There had to be a problem – and there was.

John Duncan was an honest man, but he needed money. He had children to look after. He was ready to do anything, and his bosses knew it.

They gave him the job because he couldn't say no; he couldn't afford to be honest. And the job was like a poison inside him. It changed him and blinded him, so that he couldn't see the real poison – until it was too late.

# Skyjack!

TIM VICARY

When a large plane is hijacked, the Prime Minister looks at the list of passengers and suddenly becomes very, very frightened.

There is a name on the list that the Prime Minister knows very well – too well. There is someone on that plane who will soon be dead – if the hijackers can find out who he is!

And there isn't much time. One man lies dead on the runway. In a few minutes the hijackers will use their guns again. And the Prime Minister knows who they are going to kill.

# Wyatt's Hurricane

DESMOND BAGLEY

*Retold by Jennifer Bassett*

Hurricane Mabel is far out in the Atlantic Ocean and moving slowly northwards. Perhaps it will never come near land at all. But if it hits the island of San Fernandez, many thousands of people will die. There could be winds of more than 250 kilometres an hour. There could be a huge tidal wave from the sea, which will drown the capital city of St Pierre. Mabel will destroy houses, farms, roads, bridges . . .

Only one man, David Wyatt, believes that Mabel will hit San Fernandez, but nobody will listen to him . . .

71

# Frankenstein

MARY SHELLEY

*Retold by Patrick Nobes*

Victor Frankenstein thinks he has found the secret of life. He takes parts from dead people and builds a new 'man'. But this monster is so big and frightening that everyone runs away from him – even Frankenstein himself!

The monster is like an enormous baby who needs love. But nobody gives him love, and soon he learns to hate. And, because he is so strong, the next thing he learns is how to kill . . .

# Death of an Englishman

MAGDALEN NABB

*Retold by Diane Mowat*

It was a very inconvenient time for murder. Florence was full of Christmas shoppers and half the police force was already on holiday.

At first it seemed quite an ordinary murder. Of course, there are always a few mysteries. In this case, the dead man had been in the habit of moving his furniture at three o'clock in the morning. Naturally, the police wanted to know why. The case became more complicated. But all the time, the answer was right under their noses. They just couldn't see it. It was, after all, a very ordinary murder.